Cats Rule!

The Rules,
Wisdom, and Witticisms
That Go Along with Being a Cat

illustrations
Setsu Broderick

as told to Bob Lovka

Ruth Berman, editor-in-chief
Nick Clemente, special consultant
Book design and layout by Michele Lanci-Altomare and Victor W. Perry

Library of Congress Cataloging-in-Publication Data

Lovka, Bob, Date.
   Cats rule! : the rules, wisdom, and witticisms that go along with
 being a cat / as told to Bob Lovka ; illustrations by Setsu
 Broderick.
      p.   cm.
   ISBN 1-889540-31-5 (softcover : alk. paper)
   1. Cats--Humor.   I. Title.
 PN6231.C23L687 2000
 818'.5407--dc21

                                                          00-39296
                                                           CIP

BowTie™ Press
3 Burroughs
Irvine, California 92618

Manufactured in the United States of America
First Printing November 1998
10 9 8 7 6 5 4 3 2 1

For Niner, the sweetest and bravest of all,
and life number three —B. L.

For Kyle, Raulie, Genna, Parker, and Wyatt —S. B.

Humm ! ! !

Contents

Introduction

Have you had a good talk with your cat lately?

After years of feeding cats, rescuing cats, and having cats plop down onto my computer keys or execute a full body sprawl over an open research book, I became obsessed with the answer to one burning question: *Why?* Why do cats do what they do? What are they thinking behind that nonchalant stare as you squat down stupidly wiggling some $5.95 cat toy, and they turn and saunter away to go play with a bug?

Luckily, my cat, Sonny (writing later in this book under the pen name "Sunny") grew weary of my periodic frustrations and stupid cat toys, and laid down the law...literally.

I found out that just as we humans are subject to the whims of Murphy's Law *(If anything can go wrong, it will)*, cats have their own set of irrefutable rules and laws that explain why things are the way they are between cats and people. There is even a Bill of Rights for things like being finicky over food!

Fortified by this astounding discovery, I asked a few friends if their cats jumped onto the breakfast table and deposited themselves smack dab in the middle of the

morning newspaper (an action, as I learned, that was mandated by *The Third Rule of Feline Location)* or sought out the sunniest windowsill and parked there for most of the day *(Tiarra's Necessary Correlation Between Sun and Sills)*.

People agreed. There was definitely something going on.

Thus, this book. In an effort to bridge the gap between what cats are thinking and what we think they're thinking, Sonny (Sunny) rounded up a few cohorts—Magellan, Tiarra, Shadow, and Niner—who agreed to write this long-needed scientific tome while taking into consideration some observations from people like you (stout-hearted, educated, book readers who know more about cats than the cats give you credit for).

The result is this scholarly compilation of all that governs the mysterious world of cats, along with some rather unnecessary (but insisted upon) comments by the authors themselves. These feline interjections will be denoted with each cat's initial.

Let the enlightenment begin.

Bob Lovka
Idyllwild, California

MAGELLAN'S
CAT CLASSIFICATION SYSTEM

There are only two classes of cats:
extraordinary and remarkable.

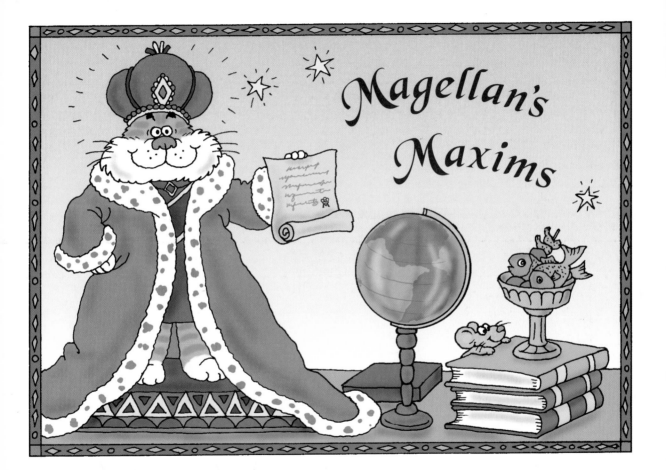

**PRIMARY LAW
OF THE GARDEN**
Butterflies are free.

Why should they cost anything?
~M

MY CATNIP

OFF LIMITS!

MAGELLAN'S FIRST MAXIM
Food and water belong to the world, but
catnip is mine alone.

MARK TWAIN'S LAW
Crossing a man with a cat will
improve the man but deteriorate the cat.

Hear! Hear! And Amen! ~M

**FIRST LAW
OF FELINE
PREROGATIVE**
A cat never goes out
the door the first time
you open it.

**MARY MARGARET'S
LAW OF FELINE MOBILITY**
If it moves, chase it.

FIRST LAW OF CAT TOYS
The more elaborate the toy the less your cat will play with it.

Much as I hate to admit it, nothing beats a paper bag or a ball of yarn!

~M

THE ATTITUDE AXIOM
Dogs are optimists.
Cats are realists.

SUNNY'S OPTIMISTIC REBUTTAL TO THE ATTITUDE AXIOM
Where there's rain, there's still someplace dry.

What is so optimistic about a species that licks feet, buries bones, and stands out in the rain?

~M

THE QUALITATIVE COMPARISON OF OPTIMISM AND PESSIMISM OCCURRING IN DOGS AND CATS
A dog believes that life is as good as it can be! A cat hopes that isn't true.

MAGELLAN'S FIRST LAW OF LIFE
Any sleep missed today can be made up tomorrow.

MR. SHEATH'S COMMENT ON THE DIFFERENCE BETWEEN CATS AND DOGS

There is no such thing as cat obedience school.

APRIL'S REBUTTAL
Just because the cat does what she wants, doesn't mean she's in charge!

Well, we do have our Principle of Feline Accommodation, which reminds us that no human wants to be shown up. Play the obedience game once in a while.

~M

MS. WALKER'S SCIENTIFIC THEORY OF CAT BEHAVIOR
In matters of attitude and action, a cat's "consistent" should be taken as "variable."

Cats exhibit only one type of behavior~distinct!
~M

MAGELLAN'S UNIVERSAL RULE OF CURIOSITY
No cat can leave well enough alone.

FIRST PRINCIPLE OF FELINE PHYSICS

Random strands of white cat hair tend to drift toward the nearest black dress.

PRIMARY PRINCIPLE OF FELINE GOOD SENSE

If it's a group, deal with it.
If it's a committee, avoid it.

While bugs dance, cats watch

—Milo the Poet

MAGELLAN'S BILL OF RIGHTS
FOR CATS:

ARTICLE **1:** All cats are born adorable, but some more so than others.

ARTICLE **2:** Each cat has the inalienable right to dig in the garden of his or her choice.

ARTICLE **3:** All cats have the right to a clean litter box.

ARTICLE **4:** Each cat has the right of refusal to come when called.

ARTICLE **5:** Yawning and stretching luxuriously at any time of day is a birthright for all felines.

ARTICLE 6: In the matters of food, the right to be finicky is hereby recognized.

ARTICLE 7: All cats, especially the longhaired, have the right to shed hair here, there, and everywhere.

ARTICLE 8: All cats are granted the right to wash in public.

ARTICLE 9: Each cat has the right to leave a household without warning, wander a few days, be adventurous, then return home and act as if nothing had happened.

ARTICLE 10: All cats at all times have the universal right to remain unbound by any laws, rules, or conventions—including these.

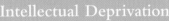

Many cats think they're smarter than dogs. Others instinctively know it!

~M

MAGELLAN'S MATHEMATICAL FORMULA FOR THE DOG

Intellectual Deprivation
+ Uncalled-for Elation
+ Abundant Defecation
= Dog

INTERNATIONAL CAT COURT TRIBUNAL RULING JS-1513

Humans who dress felines in anything more than a collar shall be liable for damages to dignity and fined under the Ludicrous Activities Law.

MAGELLAN'S GUIDE TO NUTRITION

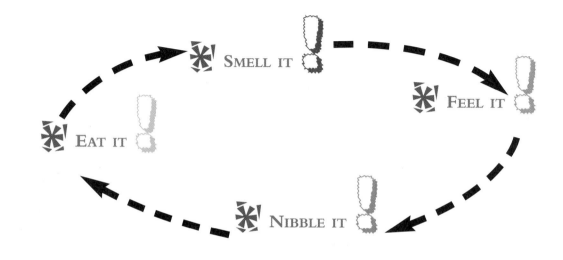

SMELL IT

FEEL IT

EAT IT

NIBBLE IT

All cats have a sixth sense~ this one's the seventh! ~M

JANA'S THEORY OF TRICKS AND TALENTS

The best trick a cat does is a disappearing act when a medication is due.

MAGELLAN'S METAPHOR

Cats don't rent, they own.

HARRIET'S HOUSEHOLD HOMILY

The cat is most attracted to the guest most allergic to him.

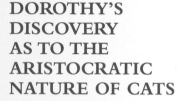

DOROTHY'S DISCOVERY AS TO THE ARISTOCRATIC NATURE OF CATS
No self-respecting cat will claw a cheap carpet.

THE FELINE FAIRNESS RULE FOR HUMANS
Whoever gets to the bed first has choice of sides.

MAGELLAN'S WARNING TO TROUBLESOME DOGS
Remember, lions are cats too.

Milo's Ode to the Owner of an Ankle-Biting Cat

Where mice are scarce
And birds, "No-No!"
Where things don't bounce or swing.
Your housebound cat
Feels kinda flat...
He needs some stimulating.

There must be a hunt!
A pounce!
An attack!
To see the long day through.
So you must understand—
Though it's not really planned—
Your ankle will have to do!

—Milo the Poet

X-TREME CAT SPORTS★

1. The crouching leap out of the clothes hamper

2. The high-flying pounce from above

3. The bolting daredevil hit-and-run at a passing ankle

★ *Fully sanctioned by the Kitty Cat Olympics Committee*

THE HOUSEHOLD COMFORT COROLLARY

Never lie on the floor when you can lie on the couch. Never lie on the couch when you can lie on the bed.

THE APPEARANCE PARADOX

No two identical cats are alike.

**THIRD PRINCIPLE OF
FELINE BEHAVIOR**
Silence is golden.

**DOROTHY'S
DISCOVERY**
If you buy something all cats
are sure to like, your cat is sure
not to like it.

**MAGELLAN'S
MAJOR MEWSING**
To spray or not to spray,
that is the question.

JULIA'S OBSERVATION OF PEOPLE WITH CATS
There's your way, my way, and the cat's way.

In the long run, it's simplest to do it the cat's way!

~M

In Praise of Cats

Friendly, nervous, introverted, or bold,
Cats are all different
As you may have been told.

Burmese are affectionate,
Somali, a bit shy,
Abyssinian, good-tempered,
But I think that's a lie!

Longhaired, shorthaired,
Tortoiseshell, spotted, or smoke,
Individual artworks
From one masterstroke!

Siamese are such big mouths!
Balinese, a little less so.
The Bombay likes people.
Vans and Rexes are on the go.

—Milo the Poet

MOTHER NATURE'S FIVE BEST GARDEN TOYS

1. Tall, springy flower stalks

 2. Out-of-reach butterflies
 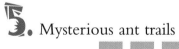

  3. Empty snail shells

4. Windblown zigzagging leaves

 5. Mysterious ant trails

**FIRST LAW OF
FELINE LOCATION**
The cat must always be
someplace else.

**MAGELLAN'S
LAW FOR
HUMANS**
Don't push it.

PRIMARY LAW OF SUNBATHING

Catch the breeze in your whiskers;
let the sun warm the bridge of your nose.

**FIRST LAW OF
FELINE INERTIA**
Start with a stretch.

**THE GUIDING RULE FOR
HOUSEHOLD MISCHIEF IN
MULTIPET DWELLINGS**
Make things difficult for
the bird and impossible
for the dog.

**SUNNY'S
PETTING
PRINCIPLE**
Not too much.
Not too often.
You'll know when.

**THE
HOUSECAT
AGENDA**
There's always one
more nap to take.

WENDY'S DEFINITION
A birdbath is that which is
incessantly watched.

**THE
WISE CAT'S
PARADOX**
At times, things
look better from
your back.

FIRST PARADOXICAL PRINCIPLE OF GROOMING
Maintain a healthy coat by rolling in dirt whenever possible.

In a Cat's Eye

*A cat doesn't stare
Into empty space.
She's watching angels
Hover in place....*

—Milo the Poet

UNIVERSAL FELINE RESPONSE TO BEING TAUGHT TRICKS
Go do it yourself.

THE FELINE COMMUNICATION COMMISSION REGULATIONS

The F.C.C. sets standards and governs communication between cats and other species. These standards are normally published in a pamphlet and distributed to members of the dog, bird, squirrel, frog, and snake communities. Simple, straightforward communications occur in most instances.

Regarding communication with humans, however, the agency was forced to painstakingly develop a hardbound volume of rules, regulations, explanations, and requirements. Whether this is due to the feline's decision not to speak, or the human's overwhelming disposition to speak and make noise at all times, remains for the reader to ponder. Here is a sample:

F.C.C. REGULATION C-101 *(Page 115):*
There is no known translation of the human words, *no, don't,* and *stop it.* Ignore them.

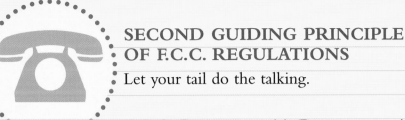

SECOND GUIDING PRINCIPLE OF F.C.C. REGULATIONS

Let your tail do the talking.

F.C.C. DIRECTIVE 14, PARAGRAPH 4 ON "ADDITIONAL COMMUNICATIONS" *(Amended June 1998)*

Human communication can also take on the strange form of sitting for hours in front of lighted boxes known alternately as television and computer. These boxes appear to be the human version of silent communication. Humor your human. Stare with them for short periods of time. Try not to yawn.

F.C.C. REGULATION C-103

In answering a command, request, or a direct human order felines are to reflect, not genuflect.

HUMAN TERMS AND USAGE GUIDE UPDATES

The F.C.C. also maintains and updates the *Feline Standard Terms and Usage Guide*, which aids in clarifying human verbal communication. The Guide is issued quarterly because humans continue to say the darndest things.

Some recent entries:

2320: G-RR-R-A-U-GHHH!
The sound humans make while playing golf.

2201: MAKING THE BED
An activity best described as creating ripples and tunnels in bedding materials that felines are to run under.

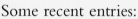

2321: ⋆%%#@#!##⋆
The term humans use while playing golf.

THE UNFORTUNATE THIRD LAW OF LIVING WITH HUMANS

The less you can tolerate human baby talk, the more it will be directed at you.

SECOND RULE OF FELINE PREROGATIVE

If it doesn't come naturally, don't do it.

SUNNY'S ATTITUDE REGARDING CANINE INTELLIGENCE

Every dog has some grand plan that will never work.

GUIDELINES FOR SURVIVING IN THE HUMAN WORLD

We've heard the human world described as "dog eat dog," heard humans ask each other, "Whattsamatter, cat got your tongue?" (No thanks!), and found that humans can *eat like pigs*, *fly the coop*, and *pull the wool* over other people's eyes. Will you please get your metaphors straight? If it's this confusing listening to you, imagine how confusing it is living with you! Thankfully, over the centuries cats have developed some rules of thumb to guide us through your unusual world.

Here are the latest, ever-evolving guidelines, customs, and advice handed down to cats living in a human world:

1. Find the highest perch and sit there.

2. An open book or spread-out papers are a human's invitation for you to plop down onto the middle of them.

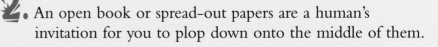

3. Whenever possible, walk upon the keyboard of a home computer. It's good luck.

4. Immediately investigate any human object not found in its "normal" place, or any object moved from one location to another.

5. If it is round, small, and on the floor, it must be swatted.

6. Stare into space for periods of time. Humans view this as mysterious.

7. Always leave word for household mice to play while you're away.

SUNNY'S FIRST LAW OF THE OUTDOORS
Birds are meant to be studied. Flies call for a quick attack.

SUNNY'S SECOND LAW OF THE OUTDOORS
The outdoors looks better from the indoors than the indoors looks from the outdoors.

SUNNY'S HOUSEHOLD IDEOLOGY
The higher the shelf the better the challenge.

MS. GILLETTE'S REFLECTION
Cats know your secrets but keep them to themselves.

**ABBREVIATED
RULES OF THE HUNT**
Slink – run – pause;
Then, slink – run – claws!

THE HOUSECAT COALITION'S
FIVE BEST PLACES TO HIDE
DURING A THUNDERSTORM

1. Under a bed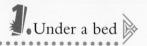

2. Deep inside a clothes closet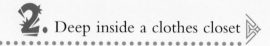

3. Under a sofa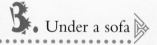

4. Behind a basement furnace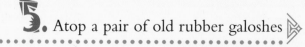

5. Atop a pair of old rubber galoshes

FIRST EXCEPTION TO THE RULE OF FELINE CONSISTENCY

Nothing is done always.

THE ELEVENTH AMENDMENT

A human toe twitching
under a bedspread is fair game
to chase and attack.

To Sit or not to Sit

For each human,
The want of a throne
Is what a chair fulfills.
For each cat,
In need of the same
It's the windowsill.

—Milo The Poet

SECOND PHILOSOPHICAL RULE OF CAT BEHAVIOR

Cats don't look *at* people, they look *into* them.

THE THREE BIGGEST LIES
HUMANS TELL TO CATS

1. 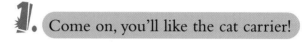 Come on, you'll like the cat carrier!

2. I'm not going to bathe you, just brush you.

3. You will absolutely love this new food!

SUNNY'S DISCOVERY
A soft, chubby tummy encased in a sweatshirt makes a great place for a nap-and-knead session.

Milo's Profoundly Spiritual Poem for Humans

You have treasures, possessions, and just plain stuff
From the mundane to the crème de la crème;
List all of the things you really need—
A dog isn't one of them!

—Milo The Poet

THIRD RULE OF FELINE LOCATION

Any human act of spreading a newspaper, book, chart,
graph or report across a sofa, desk, or tabletop requires that
a cat relocate to occupy that same space.

BOBBI'S THEORY OF RELATIVITY

Where there is one cat in a household, there soon will be at least one more.

That's because love multiplies!

~9

mmmeoow

NINER'S FIRST THEORY FOR FELINES

It's not what you say that's important, it's how you deliver the *meow*.

GRETA GARBO'S INSIGHT INTO CATS
[They] want to be alone.

Except when we demand attention!

~9

NINER'S THEORY OF GROOMING
One good lick deserves another.

9er

MS. EDWARDS'S OBSERVATION

Any pair of shoes left out of the closet will, in the eyes of a cat, become a suitable fortress from which to attack ankles and feet.

That goes for chair legs, plant pots, and bushes, too!

~9

NINER'S OBSERVATION

Anything is easier to do than undo.

THE FELINE WARNING SYSTEM

The curious culture that makes up the society of cats has a warning system that serves us well. Sometimes, we even listen to it!

 Use caution with any species other than your own.

Steer clear of small, untamed creatures known as children.

 Shots are meant to be tolerated. Baths are not.

 Stay out of rain, snow, and the microwave.

Stop, look, listen for humans before napping in a laundry basket full of warm clothes.

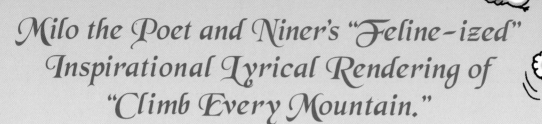

Milo the Poet and Niner's "Feline-ized" Inspirational Lyrical Rendering of "Climb Every Mountain."

1 Climb every curtain,
Dodge every flea,
Sniff every morsel,
Food is what it could be!

2 Dash down the hallway,
Leap on the bed,
Follow every ripple,
That's in the bedspread!

3 You're as free as a bird
For as long as you chase one,
Every day of nine lives
For as long as you live!

4 Climb every curtain,
Watch where you pee,
Follow your own instincts,
And live in-de-pen-dent-lyyyy!

ADRIA'S FELINE DYNAMIC CONCERNING VET BILLS AND CHRISTMAS TREES
They're easier to run up than down.

JENNIFER'S RULE FOR WORKING AT HOME
No matter how large the workspace, the cat will want to sit right on top of what's being worked on.

SIMPLIFIED BIOGENETICS OF CATS

Some cats can be Angora, some can be Russian blue, but all cats are curious.

NINER'S PHILOSOPHICAL ADVICE GOVERNING LIFE AND LEAPING FROM PLACE TO PLACE

In life and leaping, even if something looks too narrow to support you believe it will.

THE AFTERNOON LAW

When in doubt, sleep on it.

1. Appear Adorable.

NINE TIME-PROVEN HINTS FOR MANIPULATING HUMANS

2. Nap in a human lap.

3. Maintain eye contact while pleading.

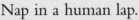

4. Confuse, confound, and astound by coming when called—one out of every four times.

5. Never explain your unexplainable side.

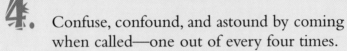

6. Use a look of innocent surprise when the dish or glass you wanted to knock off the kitchen counter does fall and break.

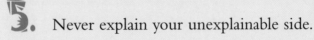

7. Claim the bed early in the evening. No human wants to disturb a curled-up, sleeping cat.

8. Allow petting.

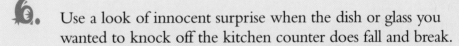

9. If you're a kitten, anything goes!

Mew!

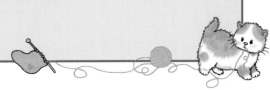

NINER'S INSPIRATION
Stairs are meant to be conquered.

FIRST RULE OF THE HUNT
Dust bunnies are acceptable prey.

KITTY YOUNGMAN'S OLDEST JOKE
A manx tells no tales.

FIRST PRECEPT OF FELINE PSYCHOLOGY
Always give in to the kitten within.

NINER'S ADVICE
Life is an adventure!
Go explore.

I told you so!

MS. BLESSER'S AXIOM
Whenever a cat causes a problem (i.e. scratching the furniture, shredding the drapes) there is a husband, boyfriend, father, or brother insisting, "I told you so!"

MARGE'S DISCOVERY
Human hands are never so interesting as when they are sewing.

Who needs
a sitter?
A cat
should be
traveling with
you!

~9

**THE PET-SITTER'S
TRUISM FOR
VACATIONING
OWNERS**
All the best sitters
are busy when
you need them.

1

APRIL'S DISCOVERY
If you feed a stray once, you will have to do it again.

2

PETER'S COMMENT
There's always one more cat.

3

JUNE'S SUMMING UP OF APRIL'S DISCOVERY AND PETER'S COMMENT
Feed a stray, adopt a family.

THIRD RULE OF FELINE GROOMING
The end of a meal calls for a full-body licking.

PAULINE'S PET THEORY
The better the petting, the louder the purr.

MELINDA'S PROFOUND CAT T-SHIRT
Hairballs Happen

THE YO-YO EFFECT
Any cat taken down from
a counter or tabletop
immediately leaps back up.

NINER'S THREE-STEP GUIDE FOR KITTENS

Humans are an odd lot. One minute it's OK for you to
sit on the couch, the next it's not.

Being a kitten gives you an advantage;
if you're even moderately cute, you
can get away with anything! Just
remember these instructions:

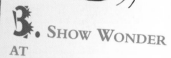

3. SHOW WONDER AT THE MUNDANE.
It's round, it rolls, it's
a ball, and you know
that. Yet, humans are
totally disarmed at the
sight of you trying to
figure out what it is
and attacking it. OK,
play along as if it's the
greatest thing since the
sardine. You can always
amuse yourself on
the Internet.

1. ACCENTUATE YOUR FUZZINESS.
Humans can't get
angry at anything that
looks soft, is round, and
has eyes. If you can put
up with the baby talk,
you'll go a long way in
training them.

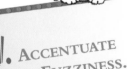

2. FALL OVER YOUR FEET AND TUMBLE A LOT.
Do this often
enough and they'll
carry you anywhere.

SECOND LAW OF SUNBATHING
A flowerbed stays cool on hot summer days.

THE HAPPY HOUSECAT'S RULE NO. 1
Anything that dangles is fair game.

You haven't lived until you've played with spaghetti hanging off a fork!

~9

FIRST POSTULATE FOR FERAL CATS
Any territory that can be marked will be marked.

NINER'S PROVERB
A rub under the chin is worth two on top of the head.

NINER'S TRUISM FOR CATS
There is no such thing as a small yawn.

NINER'S ADDITION
Often.

NINER'S NINE INSIGHTS FOR STAYING IN TOUCH WITH THE INNER KITTEN

Having nine lives makes for confusion. It's hard to remember even what you're supposed to forget. So imagine having eighteen inner kittens running around in your psyche—nine for the adjusted you, and nine for the wounded you!

Now you know why we value being alone. Even so, cat psychologists recommend we stay in touch with our inner kittens, no matter how many there are. To climb through this internal family tree, I use this guide:

1. Know thyselves, or at least know where to look.

2. To communicate from deep within takes only a tiny "mew" from without.

3. The ball of string, the paper bag, the dangling rope, the things unseen yet swiped at through the crack under the bathroom door, these are the joys of the universe.

4. It is written that cats shall inherit the earth. But no one knows if that includes Cleveland.

5. The road to enlightenment consists of two left turns, three potholes and a one-way street. Yield with caution.

6. Nothing is for certain except death and yearly booster shots.

7. Take time to smell the catnip.

8. Profound knowledge is all around, and *All around* are the first two words of "Pop Goes the Weasel."

9. Life is an open book. Lie down upon it.

10. Live by the first nine

TIARRA'S PHYSICAL AND PHILOSOPHICAL DISCOVERY

There's more to the rose bush than the rose.

Try it, I won't like it!

~T

FIRST LAW OF IMPROVEMENT

Changing the cat's food to a more nutritious and expensive kind shall result in the food being rejected at first offering.

FIRST FACT OF LIVING WITH FELINES

There's no such thing as "spoiling the cat."

I am not spoiled; I simply deserve the best.

-T

TIARRA'S REPHRASING OF MAE WEST

To err is human, never feline.

THE FIVE-MINUTE RULE
(a.k.a. The Revolving Door Maxim)

Within five minutes of coming inside, a cat shall want to go back outside. Within five minutes of being put outside, a cat shall want to come back inside.

Reflections on Feline Self-Sufficiency

People ask,
How do cats
Live so self-sufficiently?
For it could be said,
From tail to head,
Cats do act quite efficiently.
To this I say,
Throughout time
The genus Felis
In all its aristocracy,
Shows common sense,
Never gets tense,
And won't put up with bureaucracy!

—Milo the Poet

TIARRA'S FELINE/CANINE COMPARISON
Whereas cats are violins, dogs are kazoos.

TIARRA'S BEHAVIORAL THEORY
Life never reveals all its mischievous possibilities to a reasonable cat.

SHEILA'S DISCOVERY
The more expensive the curtains, the more likely they will be used as scratching posts.

FRANCINE'S FELINE MEDICAL THEORY
In treating similar ailments affecting cats and owners, the cost of the veterinary services will exceed the cost of the human medical services.

H.P. LOVECRAFT'S OBSERVATION
The cat exists as the symbol of perfect beauty.

My sentiments exactly!   ~T

TIARRA'S BUSINESS AXIOM
When it comes to business, cats mind their own.

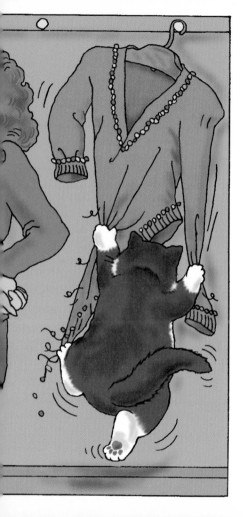

TIARRA'S UNIVERSAL RULE
Stretch everything but the truth.

Cats aren't as flexible as politicians in this matter, and we don't jump from position to position either!

-T

THE TIME-SAVER'S RULE FOR LOCATING A CAT

The first place to look for a cat is the last place you would want her to be.

MAINTAINING THE PROPER IMAGE

Cats have a long, glorious tradition and powerful mystique to uphold. While dogs sprawl all over the ground and drool or dig just about anyplace—face it, they're dogs—cats perch elegantly on windowsills and maintain dignity in all contact with humans. Even a common alley cat wouldn't be caught dead digging up an old bone in the dirt and treating it like a prize! In matters of prey and found treasure, cats proudly present their trophies to an admiring, although somewhat squeamish, human audience. It's a matter of good taste and superior breeding. Which brings us to an essential part of being a cat—those handy helpful guidelines we know as The Rules of Image. If you value codes of honor and proper behavior, you will certainly appreciate them in any cat with whom you spend time. Dignity, honor, tolerance, and unflappability are hallmarks of feline existence. You can call that *image* if you want to.

1. No matter what you do, look important doing it.

2. Walk regally and carry an uplifted tail.

3. It's not the prey or prize that is important, it's the presentation.

4. Silence is golden, but speak with authority in matters of food and outdoor access.

5. Indulging a human by participating in interactive play or showing interest in a new toy shall not exceed 45 seconds in time.

6. In matters of knocking human possessions off a shelf, countertop, or wall: stop, stare for a moment, then go about your business as if nothing happened. Repeat as necessary.

7. Do not engage in human arguments. Humans are difficult to understand and impossible to correct. Vacate the premises.

8. Maintain a straight face toward any human who attempts to communicate with you in *mews* and *meows*. Tolerate them with dignity; they're doing the best they can. You can laugh later.

9. Groom. Groom. Groom.

10 A spoonful of image goes further than a cup of performance.

FIRST LAW OF DISCERNMENT

If it came from a pet store, it will not be as comfortable as if it came from a furniture store.

If cats were authors, they would all write mysteries.

—Milo the Poet

APPROVED THINGS-TO-KNEAD LIST

 1. The human chest, stomach, and lap

 2. Afghan blankets

3. Down comforters

4. Clean laundry

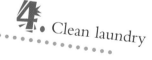 **5.** Terrycloth bathrobes

**FIRST LAW OF
FELINE INGENUITY**
There's always a clever way to do it.

**TIARRA'S
EXPLANATION**
For a cat, there is no right
way or wrong way—only
possibilities.

**CARDINAL
RULE OF
FELINE
ETIQUETTE**
Any meal calls for
a lick afterward.

PAULETTE'S DEPICTION
Cats move to a mystery all their own.

Or as Carl Sandburg put it, "the fog comes on little cat feet."

~T

JANA SUE'S SEVEN REASONS WHY
IT'S LESS FRUSTRATING TO LIVE WITH CATS THAN MEN

 Cats rarely drive you to Prozac.

 Cats keep their potty area tidy or will do something about it if it isn't.

 Cats appreciate chubby thighs. A bigger lap is a more comfortable lap.

4. Cats are constantly well groomed.

 5. Cats know it makes no sense to argue.

 6. Cats are better about going to a doctor.

 7. Cats don't snore.

JULIE'S EXPERIENCE
The cat never asks a dumb question.

Of course not. We already know everything worth knowing!

~T

CARLA'S BEDTIME MAXIM
FOR SINGLES WITH CATS

Leave the bedroom door open,
and you will never sleep alone.

TIARRA'S LAMENT

You always find something great to scratch immediately after having your claws trimmed.

KITTY'S CAT BUMPER STICKER
Tortoiseshells move more slowly than any other cat.

TIARRA'S PROVERB
Modesty is the best policy.

**FELINE THEORY
OF HOUSEHOLD
EXISTENTIALISM**
No matter the place,
you need your own
personal space.

**CARLA'S
CONCLUSION**
The main difference
between cats and men is
that you can always
trust a cat.

**TIARRA'S
ADVICE**
Be obedient—but
only when it's in
your best
interest.

**1.** Albacore tuna

TIARRA'S FINICKY FIVE-STEP FOOD PRESENTATION PHILOSOPHY

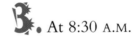**2.** Room temperature

3. At 8:30 A.M.

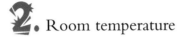**4.** On a crystal platter

**5.** Served with the left hand

Cats and babies don't know what they want, but both know what they don't want!

−T

TIARRA'S NONSEXIST RULE OF BEHAVIOR
No matter the law, rule, custom, or authority a cat will do as he or she pleases.

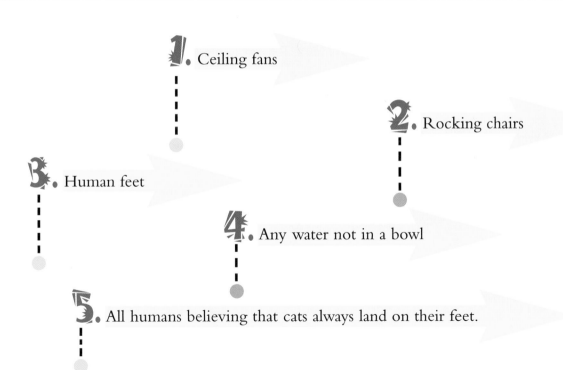

THE HAPPY HOUSECAT'S TOP FIVE THINGS TO AVOID

1. Ceiling fans

2. Rocking chairs

3. Human feet

4. Any water not in a bowl

5. All humans believing that cats always land on their feet.

TIARRA'S NECESSARY
CORRELATION BETWEEN SUN AND SILLS
The windowsill with the best sun at any moment in time is the recommended one to occupy.

Oh Where, Oh Where Is That Cat?

The key,
You see,
To a cat's locality
Is to search first
In the place
Of least accessibility!

—Milo the Poet

SHADOW'S PROVERB
A bird in the hand is impossible
with a bell on your collar.

**FIRST RULE OF
FELINE WISDOM**
The wise cat knows that it is best
to avoid perfection.

SHADOW'S DISCOVERY

It's easier to run up a telephone pole than it is to run down a telephone pole.

ERIKA'S CLARIFICATION

If the cat appears to listen and does what you command, she misunderstood whatever you were saying.

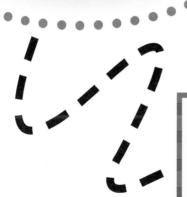

FELINE RULE OF MOBILITY

Before taking any action, sleep on it.

SHADOW'S FIVE SUGGESTIONS FOR HUMANS TO IMPROVE A CAT'S LIFE

3. There's no better pillow than a bedroom pillow. Be generous. Most cats are willing to share.

2. Cats and rain don't mix. Get rid of it!

4. Be sure the veterinarian's hands are warm.

1. Outlaw the use of bells on cat collars.

5. Tuna! Tuna! Tuna!

JOY'S CAT-TO-FOOD EQUATION
You can lead a cat to dinner, but you can't make her eat.

SHADOW'S DEFINITION
A catnap is the time a cat naps between sleeping periods.

SHADOW'S LAW OF TIMING
Be the first one onto the bed and the last one off it.

A word to the wise
From one who cares:
Keep your tail away
From rocking chairs!

—Milo the Poet

THE OLD HIPPY CAT'S SLOGAN
Never trust anybody who's clothes don't collect cat hair.

SHADOW'S FIRST THEORY OF SHELF-WALKING

Nothing knocked from a shelf ever reaches the floor without knocking down something else.

THE FELINE TIME EQUATION FOR HUMANS

If it's your free time, it must be my petting time.

WILLIAM BURROUGHS' OBSERVATION
The cat does not offer services. The cat offers itself.

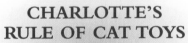

CHARLOTTE'S RULE OF CAT TOYS
The cheapest toy will outlast the most expensive one.

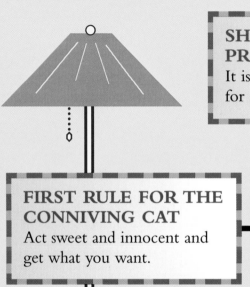

SHADOW'S PRECEPT
It is never too early for a morning nap.

FIRST RULE FOR THE CONNIVING CAT
Act sweet and innocent and get what you want.

SECOND RULE FOR LIVING IN DUAL-PET HOMES

Let sleeping dogs lie.

SHADOW'S THIRD LAW

Run as you must, but especially run amok.

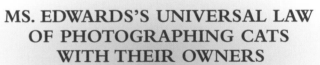

MS. EDWARDS'S UNIVERSAL LAW OF PHOTOGRAPHING CATS WITH THEIR OWNERS

The best shot of the cat is the worst shot of the owner.
The best shot of the owner is the
worst shot of the cat.

MS. EDWARDS'S FIRST LAW OF PET PHOTOGRAPHY

The most lovable pose will be ruined when the cat jumps as the flash goes off.

MS. EDWARDS'S SECOND LAW OF PET PHOTOGRAPHY

When the setup, lighting, and pose work, the camera doesn't.

SIX THINGS CATS ARE REQUIRED BY LAW TO DO WHEN YOU'RE NOT AT HOME

1. Open and close the cabinets, sliding doors, and latches you never thought we could.

2. Run over, under, around, and through the kitchen chair.

3. Jump onto kitchen counters and sample whatever is available.

5. Explore bedroom closets and rearrange clothing dangling from hangers.

4. Step on the remote control, watch television, step and turn it off again.

6. Tip over open bags of cat food.

SHADOW'S OUTDOOR PRINCIPLE
A tree is an invitation to climb.

THE VETERINARY ASSISTANT'S LAMENT
Good-tasting cat medicine will be refused as likely as bad-tasting cat medicine.

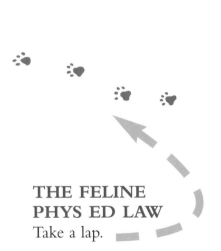

THE FELINE
PHYS ED LAW
Take a lap.

JOY'S LAW OF CATS IN THE NIGHT

Any housecat not allowed to sleep with you at night, will be sleeping either (1) at your feet; (2) next to your leg; (3) against your back; or (4) on top of you, by the next morning.

APRIL'S COROLLARY
If allowed to sleep with you,
the cat will choose to
sleep elsewhere.

Milo the Poet's Quick Guide to Human Affection

If it's a human heart you wish to trap
Simply climb upon the lap!

THIRD RULE OF CAT BEHAVIOR
Where there's a will,
there's a won't.

SHADOW'S ADAGE
Tails speak louder than words.

SHADOW'S SCHEDULE

6:00 A.M.: Wake human and go back to sleep

8:30–9:00: Morning stretch and breakfast

9:00–11:00: Post-breakfast nap

11:00–11:40: A quick forty winks

11:40–2:00 P.M.: Explorations and windowsill contemplations

(2:00–5:30): Catnap

(5:30–6:00): Pre-dinner nap

(6:00–6:00): Food survey and rejection

(6:01–6:05): Pleading for outdoors

(6:05–On): Post-dinner naps

Photo by Joy Edwards

Bob Lovka is a Southern California–based writer whose work includes poetry, satire, humor books and calendars, and television, script, and stage show writing. Bob's connection to felines and canines keeps expanding. Homeless cats and dogs look him up constantly, and uncannily they have increased their appearances since Bob wrote *The Splendid Little Book of All Things Cat* and *The Splendid Little Book of All Things Dog*. Many of these animals have found homes through Bob's association with Angel Puss and Pooch Rescue. Bob is owned by a cat and is tormented by a jealous Lhasa apso.

Photo by Rick Broderick

Setsu Broderick's illustrations, decorative designs, and commercial artwork are seen throughout the world. Her whimsical and charming original creations have been turned into collectibles, music boxes, plush toys, books, and figurines. She has illustrated two books, *The Splendid Little Book of All Things Cat* and *The Splendid Little Book of All Things Dog*. Max, her desk-chewing cockatoo, remains her most vocal art critic.